TAROT SPREADS FOR WRITERS

HOW TO USE TAROT TO ENHANCE CREATIVITY AND EMPOWER YOUR AUTHOR LIFE

KATE KRAKE

INKWELL & ELM

CONTENTS

SPREADS FOR WRITING FICTION

SPREADS FOR CHARACTER DEVELOPMENT

SPREADS FOR PLOT DEVELOPMENT

SPREADS FOR NONFICTION

INTRODUCTION

Tarot and writers are a harmonious match. The tarot is a story, an archetypal evolution from our naïve, foolish beginnings through to gathering all the wisdom of the world, and so many nuances of experience in between. Writers think in story, so even for beginning tarot practitioners, the cards already speak to us in the language we know best. This book helps to guide those conversations through a series of tarot card spreads designed especially for writers.

If this is your first foray into tarot, do not be intimidated. It is part of the Tarot Writers mission to demystify tarot and open the doors to all curious minds wanting to explore the infinite creative potential of the cards. No prior experience necessary.

THE SPREADS

A tarot spread is an arrangement of cards drawn with a specific question or premise in mind. Each a card represents a specific aspect of this premise. The meaning of a card may vary depending on its position within the spread and the surrounding cards. We go into more about these relational readings in a later section.

Some spreads see cards arranged symbolically. Tarot is a symbolic language, and the spreads can add another layer to that. Suggested spread diagrams are provided for some spreads in this book.

For other spreads, the card positions are intentionally obscure, so even if each card is ascribed a specific representation, please lay them however you like. This is intended to provide an opportunity to exercise interpretation and intuitive answers. Some spreads combine both. Ultimately, like every tarot interpretation, the arrangement of cards in any spread is up to you.

The card position labels in each spread are a guide to components of the question or premise at hand. The labels can be interpreted as freely as you like, or even completely changed if you feel something alternative would suit. In certain spreads, the labels have been made deliberately open and obscure to prompt creative and intuitive thinking.

The spreads offered in this book cover many aspects of writing and the writer's life, including creativity and ideas, the author life, story structure, and character development. There are spreads for applicable to fiction and nonfiction writers.

Some spreads are general insights and quick draws of one or two cards. Others are intricate spreads that beckon us to embark on an immersive journey of analysis, diving deep into many cards.

Writing tips accompany some spreads.

Several spreads are based on writing resources, such as formal narrative structures, guidebooks, etc. Those resources are listed in the appendix. Others are based on traditional tarot spreads. Others are entirely developed by me for my writing and life. I've used every spread in these pages in my writing life in some way at some time, even in the development of this very book.

WHAT YOU WILL NEED

To use the spreads in this book, a few things are required. Some are optional but valuable.

To read tarot, we first require an open mind. If you've picked up this book, you're likely carrying that already.

You will require a tarot deck. Any deck will suffice, although it is recommended to choose a deck with artwork that speaks to you in some personal way. Many tarot enthusiasts acquire a deck collection, using different decks to suit different moods or themes. I have different decks I like to use for different writing projects.

Time and space are also a necessity. A tarot reading is not a practice to be rushed. Reading a spread, even a single card spread, requires a calmed yet alert presence. Space refers to the physical surface to lay the cards, particularly the large intricate spreads, but also the mental space to be open to whatever a card might speak to you.

If you are new to tarot, it's recommended you start with a tarot guide book to introduce the traditional meanings of the cards. From there, you might also like to explore guides that teach intuitive reading. You will find a list of resources for learning tarot in this book.

A tarot journal is a helpful tool. Not all tarot readers will use a journal, but journaling your readings can be a valuable and insightful practice. Use your journal to record which cards are drawn in which spreads and then write about your interpretations of the cards and their relevance to you in the reading.

THE SPIRITUAL SIDE OF TAROT

This book takes a secular approach to tarot culture. I respect all spiritual beliefs about tarot, but my personal spirituality remains private and is not represented in these pages.

All work I do with Tarot Writers, including this book, focuses on the cards as creative tools, symbols steeped in eons of tradition that can help us think and feel differently, often in ways we might never have before considered. Tarot is many things for many people and only you get to decide what it means to you.

This book is offered as a guide and a conversation, not a prescription. It's ideas, not advice.

There isn't a single book or resource that can cover everything there is to know about reading tarot. That's because part of reading tarot is an exploration of unknowing. Card meanings will change depending on where and when you are in your life, and how a particular deck speaks to you, how you think and feel about the answers you're seeking, even how you feel about tarot in that moment. Spreads will speak to you differently with different decks. Be open to all of this unknowing and discovery, and let the cards lead your creativity along this ancient path of inspiration and imagination.

TAROT GLOSSARY

Tarot is a dynamic, complex and ancient system, and this glossary merely scratches the surface of its terminology. It does, however, offer a simple starting point to new practitioners.

Arcana

Arcana literally means secrets or mysteries. Standard decks have two Arcana, two sets of cards, the Major and Minor Arcana.

The Major Arcana - also called the trump cards. Typically, 22 cards representing powerful archetypal, fateful energies.

Minor Arcana - Typically comprises 56 cards divided into four suits (Wands, Cups, Swords, and Pentacles) and represents the varying nuances of day-to-day experiences.

Clarifier Card

An additional card drawn during a reading to gain further clarification on a specific issue, or to provide deeper understanding of the cards already laid out in the spread. A clarifier card is optional in every spread.

Court Cards

The Page, Knight, Queen and King cards of the Minor Arcana. The court cards represent different personality types or archetypes. They typically depict people and can indicate specific individuals or aspects of the querent's personality or external influences. Different decks can have different names for these cards.

Deck

A set of tarot cards. Decks are typically unified in a theme, artistic style, or some other element that unites the cards.

Intuitive Meaning

Every reader can bring their own interpretations of a card's meaning. This might be based on the traditional meanings combined with the reader's life experiences and views, or it might be solely from the reader's intuition and move away from tradition completely. Intuitive readings are usually inspired by the reader's response to the art and or words on the card, as well as the card's position relative to other cards in the spread.

Querent

The person for whom the reading is done. When reading for yourself, you are both the reader and the querent. Reading for a fictional character, your character is the querent. Reading for a friend, your friend is the querent.

Reader

The person performing the tarot spread and interpreting the cards. Also called the practitioner.

Reversals

When a tarot card appears upside down during a reading, it is considered a reversal. Reversals can modify or add depth to the card's traditional meanings, indicating challenges, shadow messages, or blocked energies. Some readers ignore reversals and simply flip the card the right way up.

Significator

A card chosen to represent the querent or a specific person or energy central to the reading. The significator provides additional context and serves as a focal point during the interpretation. The significator card is optional, though some spreads in this book specify its inclusion.

Spreads

Spreads are the patterns in which we lay the cards out. Just as each card has its meaning, so too can each position in a spread.

Suits

The Minor Arcana is typically divided into four suits. These are usually Wands, Cups, Swords, and Pentacles, but different decks can give suits different names. Suits are arranged like playing cards, starting from Ace, with ten numbered cards, and then court cards of Page, Knight, Queen, and King.

Each suit has its own central theme. These are:

Wands – ideas and intuition

Cups – creativity and emotion

Swords – action and logic

Pentacles – material values.

Traditional Meaning

Each tarot card holds a traditional meaning and most modern decks represent these meanings in some way in their art.

REVERSED CARDS

A reversed tarot card is where a card appears upside down. It's up to you what to do if a card is laid in the reverse. Different readers have different approaches to reversals.

Some readers disregard reversals and turn the card the right way up to continue with the reading.

Other readers use the reversal to add further depth to the card's meaning.

In some tarot guide books, reversal meanings are given as negative opposites to the card's traditional meaning, challenges to overcome. For example, the 0 card, The Fool is traditionally seen as blissful innocence, the optimistic start of a new adventure. The reversal of The Fool is then ignorance and naivety, irrational risks, and aimlessness.

Reversals can also be seen not as negative opposites, but indications where the querent might be blocked. For example, The Fool in reverse might be seen as the querent needing to embrace a sense of innocent optimism instead of taking their situation so seriously and needing to plan every detail ahead of time.

Reversals might also be seen as messages from the shadow self, that dark part we each have that we tend to keep hidden. Don't think of the shadow here as an "evil" side, but as our deepest, most private selves that even our nearest and dearest might not know.

For others, a reversal might mean the direction of energy as inward, as opposed to the outward of the upright card. For example, a reversed Fool might show that this new adventure you're about to begin might be an inward journey, not something happening in the outside world. Or it's a new venture that you're keeping private until the time is right.

A simple way to use reversals is in yes/no spreads. If you seek a yes or no answer, draw a card. Upright is yes, and the implications of that yes. Reversed is no, and the implications of that no.

There's no right way to read a card reversal, and you might change your approach from spread to spread. It's a good idea to keep to one approach per reading so as not to overly complicate things.

RELATIONAL READINGS OF TAROT SPREADS

Reading a tarot card spread can be so much more than reciting the traditional meanings of each drawn card.

Every position in the spread adds its own meaning to a card. We also want to look at the cards in relation to the surrounding cards, and the spread as a whole. I call this relational reading.

Example Relational Reading Spread

A three card spread on an author's strengths and weaknesses.
1. Your strengths.
2. Your weaknesses.
3. Advice on navigating the two ends.

The drawn cards are:
1. The Hermit
2. Ten of Cups
3. Three of Wands

Thinking of a person's strengths in relation to the Hermit card might indicate the querent is very good at withdrawing from the world, going inward, and getting their writing done. As this is a Major Arcana card, the meaning is deeply archetypal and speaks to more fateful things about this person. As such, we might see this as a fundamental strength, something that won't change too much.

The Ten of Cups is typically a positive card, relating to a person's love for their family, contentment, and harmonious relationships. However, as this card falls into a position asking the querent to consider weaknesses, we might think of how their commitment to their relationships might hold them back in some way. Perhaps it's family distractions, perhaps it refers to their writing community.

As this is a Minor card alongside that first Major card, we could interpret this as a weakness that is highly negotiable. Significant change is possible here. It's a minor weakness against a major strength.

The last card of the spread suggests how the two might unify. The Three of Wands is about looking outward and broadening horizons.

This might advise the querent to seek other relationships. Perhaps the querent's relationships are not as valuable as they might think. And as this is a negotiating card, perhaps it also suggests this author need not be so inwardly focused, despite it being a strength, and look outwards for ways to navigate their weaknesses.

As this is a Wands card, it's about primal energy, determination, hard work and expansion. Considering this card is a negotiation with the former Cups card, we might view it as offering guidance to prioritize logical thinking. The querent might be encouraged to focus more on the head rather than the heart and soul of the emotional nature of the Cups suit.

Overall, since this is a spread directed to an author's life, work is a big component of what's being asked here. That final negotiating advice card is about outward expansion. So we develop a sense that this draw is suggesting the querent focus on the worldly aspects of their work, the time spent in the chair, perhaps the business side of the author life.

In another spread, in other positions, these three cards might take on entirely different meanings. So proceed slowly with each spread, taking time to not only consider what the cards themselves mean but also how they relate to one another in the context of what the spread is specifically asking.

OTHER SUGGESTIONS FOR INTERROGATING CARD RELATIONSHIPS

How are any archetypal character cards (Court cards in the Minors, or Major Arcana cards 0-5) facing one another?

How are any unnamed people in other cards positioned in relation to one another?

What might one card say to its neighbor?

Are there any visual links between cards? E.g. Repeated animals, flowers, tools, sigils, colors, etc.

Are there any opposites in the symbols on the drawn cards? E.g. water and fire, male and female, sky and earth, black and white, etc.

Do you have any reversals? Might a reversed card be blocking a neighboring card?

When first starting out with tarot, many practitioners begin by just combining the traditional meanings with the labelled card position. Intricate relational readings develop as we familiarize ourselves with the cards and get to know the decks we are working with. Like all things related to tarot reading, work at your own pace in the method that feels most comfortable to you and let your practice develop organically.

QUICK GENERAL
SPREADS

SINGLE CARD DRAWS

There is no simpler spread than the single card draw. It's just one card. Yet, despite this simplicity, single cards spread can take on great and powerful meanings.

You might like to draw your single cards in the morning, musing on them throughout the day and observing how the card's meaning might appear as you go about your life.

Drawing at night is also a good idea. The card can be a reflection of the day just spent, or it might be something to consider for tomorrow, letting the undercurrents of your dreams explore the card's potentials.

Here are several suggestions on how to frame a single card spread.

For the Author

- A daily card to set a theme for the day.
- A definitive answer to a specific problem.
- A daily meditation.

- Yes or no.

For the Work

- A definitive answer to a specific problem.
- A random writing prompt.
- A theme for a scene.
- A defining character trait.
- An aspiration for the coming day's work.
- An analysis of the spent day's progress.
- Yes or no.

The interpretations for single card draws are endless. You might also like to take a fully intuitive approach, draw a card and see where inspiration takes you.

THREE CARD DRAWS

Three card draws are one of the most common tarot spreads. Like single draws, the triple cards are simple but hold great creative potential.

These quick and simple spreads are constructive ways to generate solutions to problems or get an overall feel for a situation.

They are highly adaptable, able to apply to matters in your own life, or you can read them for your characters or plots.

Full Day Draw

This is a simple spread, with each card drawn over the course of the day. Select your first card in the morning, a second card in the middle of the day, and then the third in the evening. Between each draw, spend time musing on the card's significance. This might also happen subconsciously as you go about your day.

At the end of the day, reflect on the three card spread as a whole.

This spread is designed to read for your author life, but is easily adapted to suit your in-writing world, such as a character's day.

1. Morning - grounding expectations of the day's writing plans.
2. Midday - the day in progress.
3. Evening - Reflections on what you wrote today.
You may wish to add a fourth card...
4. Looking forward to tomorrow.

Strengths and Weaknesses

1. Your strengths.
2. Your weaknesses.
3. Advice on navigating the two ends.

Opportunities and Setbacks

1. Opportunities currently on offer.
2. Setbacks you perceive.
3. Outcome.

The Happy Half Way - Compromising Between Two Options

1. Nature of Option 1.
2. Nature of Option 2.
3. The happy half way compromise.

Trust Your Gut

1. Choice one.
2. Choice two.
3. Your gut feelings.

Yes No

1. The nature of the situation.
2. Benefits of saying yes.
3. Benefits of saying no.

SPREADS FOR IDEAS AND CREATIVITY

THE CREATIVE SELF

This spread delves into self-awareness and aims to illuminate aspects of the self we might not have considered as part of our inspiration process.

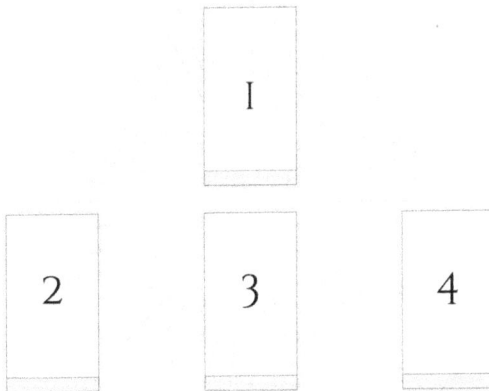

```
        +-----+
        |     |
        |  1  |
        |     |
        +-----+

+-----+   +-----+   +-----+
|     |   |     |   |     |
|  2  |   |  3  |   |  4  |
|     |   |     |   |     |
+-----+   +-----+   +-----+
```

1. Who am I?
2. What do I want?
3. What do I love?

4. What do I fear?
5. What do I think?

CREATIVE ADVANCEMENT

When we're looking to take our creativity to the next level, sometimes the best way to advance is to look backward. This spread acknowledges the milestones that have shaped your current path, the visions that took you to this point, and built your creative strengths. Where do you want to go from here? And what do you need to learn to get there?

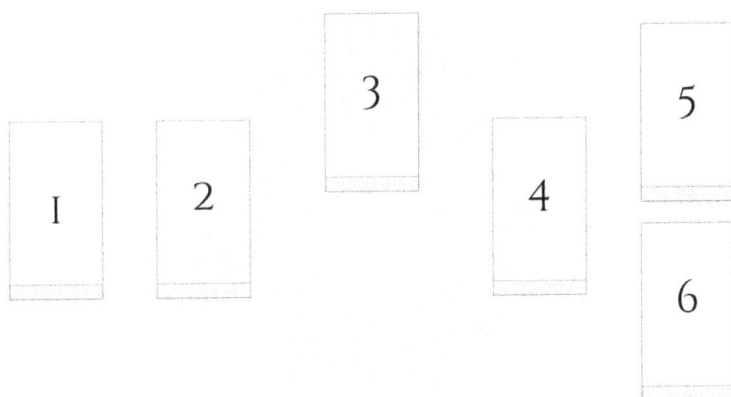

1. Past creative aspirations.

2. Past creative achievements.
3. Current creative aspirations.
4. Obstacles.
5. Assets.
6. Lessons from past failures.

CREATIVE REPLENISHMENT

Creative replenishment is a phase of the creative process we all need to enter periodically. Perhaps it's at the end of a project that you've given your all to. Perhaps you're recovering from a period of burnout. Perhaps you just need a splash of creative rejuvenation.

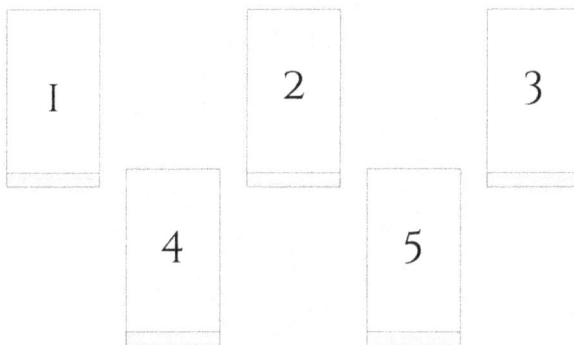

```
  ┌─────┐         ┌─────┐         ┌─────┐
  │     │         │     │         │     │
  │  1  │         │  2  │         │  3  │
  │     │         │     │         │     │
  └─────┘   ┌─────┘     └─────┐   └─────┘
            │     │     │     │
            │  4  │     │  5  │
            │     │     │     │
            └─────┘     └─────┘
```

1. Current creative energy.
2. Blocks and challenges.

3. A forgotten or overlooked passion to reconnect with.
4. Nurturing practices.
5. Your creative future.

UNBLOCKING
FROM PAST

This tarot spread encourages you to reflect on something from your history that may impact your current emotional state and hinder creativity.

It invites you to reconnect with the things you once loved and were inspired by, as well as more negative experiences of past emotion. It's not always the negative aspects of the past that can keep us blocked in the present, so we also look at positive past experiences that might be blocking the present or future.

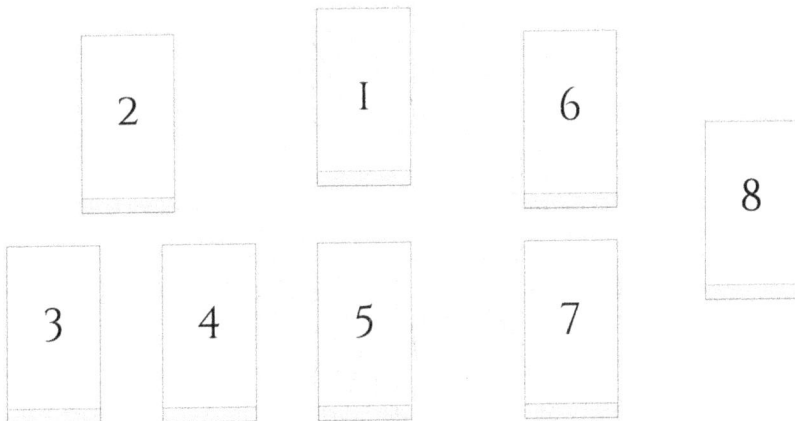

2	I	6	
			8
3	4	5	7

1. Something you love in the present.
2. Something you loved in the past.
3. Someone from your past you loved.
4. Something that once irritated you.
5. Something that once scared you.
6. A time when you felt most free.
7. A goal you used to have.
8. A present action to release the past.

UNCOVERING SUBCONSCIOUS OBSTACLES

This spread is for when you are feeling driven to create, but feel stuck or blocked, and are uncertain what's holding you back.

```
 ┌───┐
 │ 1 │
 └───┘

 ┌───┐   ┌───┐   ┌───┐
 │ 2 │   │ 4 │   │ 5 │
 └───┘   └───┘   └───┘

 ┌───┐
 │ 3 │
 └───┘
```

1. Significator (you presently).
2. The problem on the upper conscious level.
3. The problem in the deep subconscious.

4. Intuitive message from yourself.
5. First step necessary to unblock.

JOINING THE DOTS

Creativity is often a process of drawing connections between distinct elements, creating new meanings from combinations of existing ideas. As such, it is our job as creatives to fill our lives with a lot of elements.

Use this spread to evoke different ideas from different themes of life. Draw them together to create new and exciting possibilities.

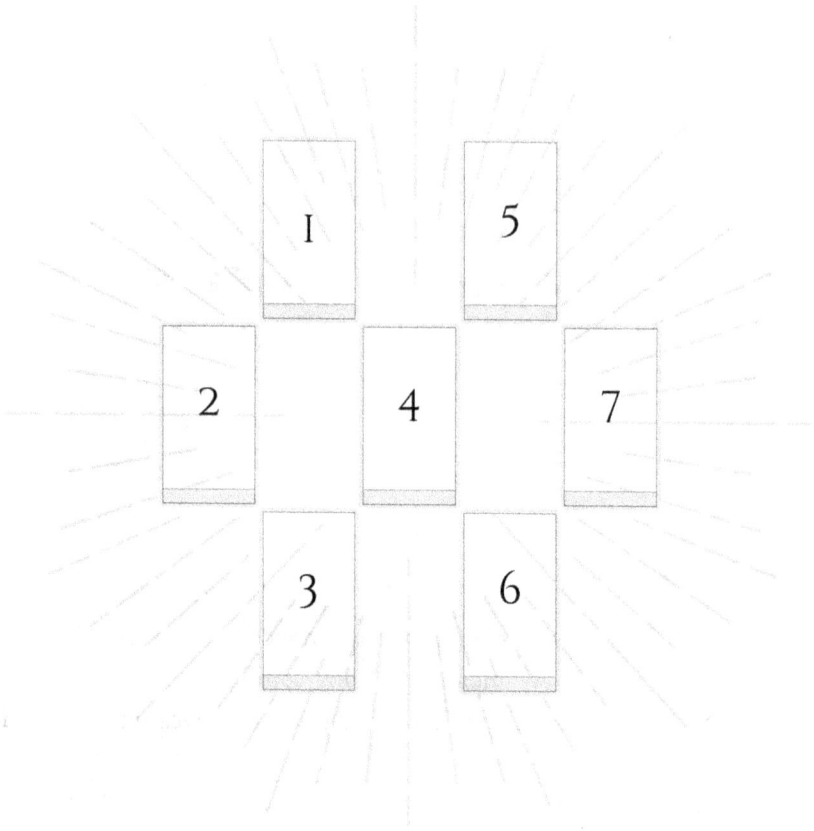

1. An aspect of your personal life you think is fascinating.
2. An aspect of someone else's personal life you think is fascinating.
3. A connection to an early memory.
4. A personal aspiration.
5. Something from the past.
6. Random thought.
7. A link drawing together positions 1 - 6.

UNEXPECTED INSPIRATION

We never know where creative inspiration will be found. Often when we're feeling blocked, it can be because we're looking for inspiration or motivation in too familiar territory. This spread offers a chance to step off the deeply trodden paths of your creative process and uncover inspiration in hidden places. Might that hidden place be right in front of you?

1. Current state of your creative life.
2. An unexpected place to seek inspiration.
3. A hidden resource within you.
4. A hidden truth in your present relationships.
5. Something obvious about your life in a new light.

MESSAGE FROM
THE MUSE

Imagine your muse is an actual entity, a spirit or person, perhaps an animal that stands alongside you while you work and ideate. Your muse knows everything about you, even things you don't know yourself, and their only wish is that you work and create to your fullest potential. Imagine your muse can see the future and understands the past with perfect clarity. Now imagine your muse is speaking directly to you through the topics in this spread.

1. Strength.
2. Weakness.
3. Ease.
4. Fear.
5. Future.
6. Truth.
7. Closing Message.

WHAT SHOULD I WRITE ABOUT?

This is the question stuck on every blank page, in the mind of every writer who stares at a flashing cursor. It's the fundamental question of creative block, yet so often we complicate its truest, most obvious answer with fear, with outside influences, and future projections that have very little if anything to do with the actual thing we want to write about. Strip all of that away and let this spread answer that most fundamental question in the most straightforward way.

1. What do I like?
2. What do I want?
3. What have I enjoyed writing about in the past?
4. What should I write about?

CREATIVE SHAKE UP

Often, our creative processes can slow, stagnate, or fall away completely simply because we do the same thing day in and day out. Creative thinking is about meaningful novelty, but how are we meant to uncover new and exciting inspirations when we don't have new and exciting thoughts? This spread prompts us to follow curiosity into a new creative territory, or discover a new offshoot on the path of our existing ways.

4

1   2   5

3

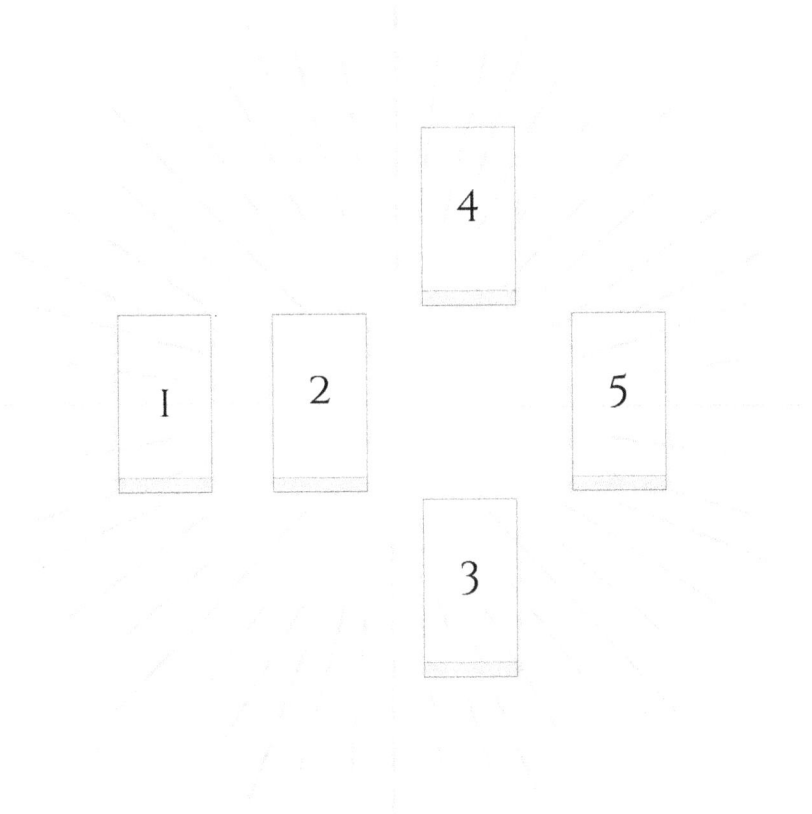

1. A creative path you've always been curious about.
2. Current creative routine.
3. Current negative patterns or habits.
4. A new perspective.
5. The path ahead.

DEALING WITH CREATIVE FOMO

The fear of missing out (FOMO) can manifest in various ways for writers. It encompasses the fear of missing opportunities to explore new ideas, riding the wave of popular social media or other industry trends, publishing in hot genres, or seizing networking chances. Creative FOMO often results in paralysis, as we become too scared or disheartened to pursue our own paths, fixated on what others are doing. This spread raises important questions about why we are looking outwards, and how what we are coveting might align with the creative paths we've already chosen.

1. Why are you looking outward?
2. What's the appeal of the other way?
3. Your current creative path.
4. Compromise between 2 and 3.

UNDERSTANDING YOUR INNATE CREATIVITY

Understanding and embracing our innate creativity is critical if we want to work in alignment with our values and our unique voices. Without the grounding of our innate creativity, we are prone to all kinds of fears and doubts that can hinder our writing or derail us all together.

Each position in this spread offers a unique perspective and exploration of your core creative self and how your creative nature has been formed over time.

1. Core creative essence.
2. Subconscious conflicts.
3. Past influences.
4. Current influences.
5. Central creative archetype.
6. Aspiration.

FICTION WRITING PROMPT

Tarot does not always have to be a deep analysis of our souls. The cards contain infinite stories ready to inspire and empower our craft.

This spread covers five basic components of story. You can use it in the most basic form and let your creativity fill in the rest, or draw additional cards for each point to inspire further details.

1. The type of story - genre, format, etc.
2. The main character.
3. A challenge for the main character.
4. Action the main character takes to overcome the challenge.
5. Outcome.

INTUITIVE CREATIVITY READING

Draw any number of cards while considering creativity in general. Let the cards speak to you freely. Don't consult any external guides.

What do the cards suggest?

SPREADS FOR THE AUTHOR LIFE

THE CELTIC CROSS FOR WRITERS

The Celtic Cross is a traditional tarot spread. Most agree that it was first used in 1911 in A.E Waite's *The Pictorial Key to the Tarot*, the guidebook that accompanied the original Rider Waite Smith deck, though it may have been in use before this publication.

Over the decades, the Celtic Cross card labels and reading order have changed and different practitioners have made their own interpretations, but the essence of the spread remains. It's a double section spread in the form of a cross within a circle, and a ladder.

The first six cards, the cross, are all about the querent's current life, while the ladder is their future progression. The ladder is not a future set in stone, but a potential if the querent continues on their present path. It's a future that can be changed with conscious effort.

1. The present situation.
2. Positive forces in your favor.
3. Potential and aspirations.
4. The subconscious.
5. The past.
6. Relationships.
7. Psychology and attitudes.
8. External environment.
9. Hopes and fears.
10. The outcome.

SHOULD I QUIT THIS PROJECT?

There are countless reasons you might feel like giving up on a writing project. A story might feel too vast, a rough draft might feel impossibly messy and daunting, you might question the market potential of an idea. Perhaps you're simply more interested in starting a different project.

Sometimes quitting is the best option. Other times, it's an easy escape from fear and doubt, and it's often impossible to tell which side your urge to quit is coming from.

This spread questions the forces that are prompting you to quit and balances them with the potential value in persisting.

1. Forces pushing you to quit.
2. Reasons to continue.
3. Reasons to quit.
4. Outcome.

SHOULD I RESTART THIS PROJECT?

Restarting a work in progress is akin to quitting altogether, but this time we're thinking about quitting the current approach to have another attempt at getting it right.

There are many reasons a writer might be prompted to tear it all down and start over. Often it's the right thing to do, equally often it's a reaction to fear and doubt. This spread looks at the value of starting over against the value of persisting within the context of your overall mindset that is coloring the conflict.

1. Current WIP status.
2. Your current mindset.
3. External forces prompting you to restart.
4. Reasons to continue without restarting.
5. Outcome.

AUTHOR BUSINESS PLAN

If writing is something more than a hobby, or you aspire for it to be, then a business plan is critical. This spread will not devise an author business plan for you, but the insights gained from considering these elements will guide you to create a plan that works for your life in a sustainable and authentic way.

1. Your life situation (family, kids, school, day job, etc.).
2. Author aspirations.
3. Author situation (new author, established author, etc.).
4. Where is your energy flowing?
5. Your current psychological state (inner influences).
6. Outside influences.
7. Long term vision.

CHOOSING BETWEEN PROJECTS

Having too many ideas is a good problem to have, but it rarely feels great to be torn by indecision. This spread prompts us to think of the pros and cons of pursuing one project over another, and offers a defining outcome to decide on your final choice.

Struggling to decide between more than two projects? Add additional cards for significators and benefits and drawbacks for as many projects as you are deciding between.

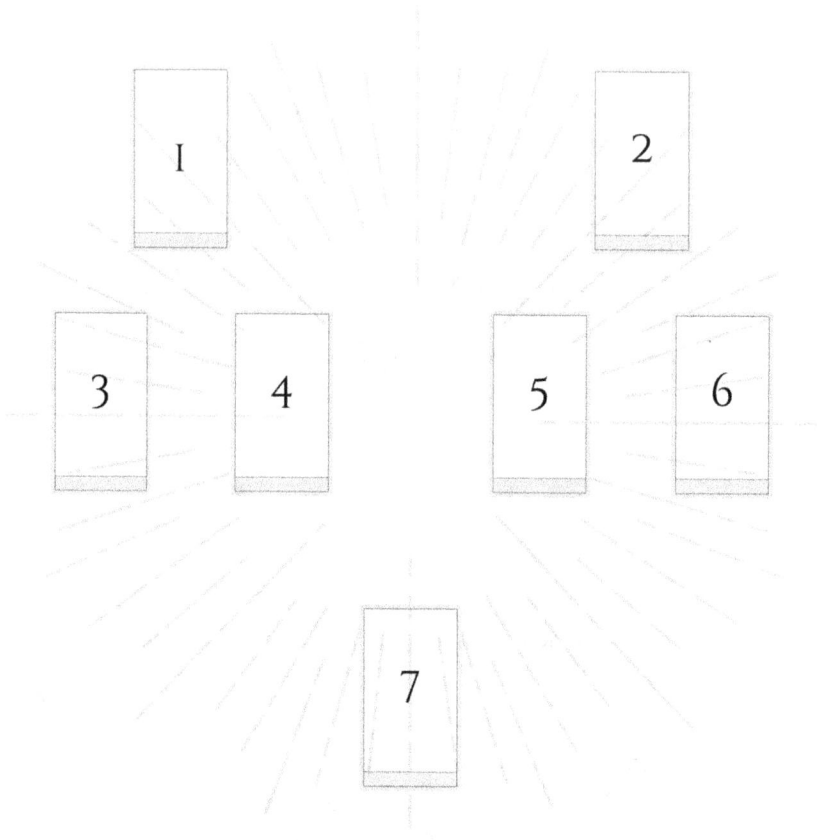

1. Significator of project 1.
2. Significator of project 2.
3. Benefits of pursuing project 1.
4. Benefits of pursuing project 2.
5. Drawbacks of pursuing project 1.
6. Drawbacks of pursuing project 2.
7. Outcome.

AM I ON THE RIGHT PATH?

This spread is for when you are working on a particular writing project and wonder if it's the best use of your energies. This could be a career based questioning, (e.g. are you working toward your optimal financial position?), or it could be a personal conversation you're having with your muse (e.g. are you serving yourself with this project?).

1. Beginning of the project in time (not the actual start of the story).
2. You now.
3. The changing you.
4. Your goal for the project.

WHERE TO FIND HELP

We all need help at some point in the writing journey. That could be help from a craft perspective, where we might consult a professional editor or trusted and qualified critique partner. It might be some help in our mindset where we might consult an author mentor, coach, or psychologist.

If you're feeling a bit (or a lot) lost, and feel you need some help, but not sure what kind of help you'll most benefit from, try this spread.

1. Significator for your project.
2. What you see as the problem.
3. Answer from your higher self (intuition).
4. Where to seek help.
5. Outcome.

EMOTIONAL WRITER'S BLOCK

Sometimes our writer's block stems from an emotional undercurrent we may or may not be aware of.

This spread helps to tap into what you're feeling and how your emotions are impacting your creative flow.

1. What am I feeling?
2. How is this feeling impacting my creativity?
3. How do I release this feeling?
4. What can I turn this feeling into?
5. What am I learning right now?

SELF CHECK IN

How are you feeling, writer?

Use this spread anytime you're feeling lost, confused about your goals and your life as a writer, or any time you are musing on your life in general.

1. Current self.
2. Key goal.
3. Current obstacles.
4. Achievements to reflect on.
5. Warnings from fears.
6. What to embrace.
7. Where to best find support.
8. Advice and encouragement.

FEELING DISHEARTENED WITH A PROJECT

Sometimes we can be writing along happily and then hit a point where we're no longer feeling good. What do we do about it? What's wrong with the work? What's wrong with us? This spread looks at the project itself and asks you to consider the context of what else is going on in your life right now.

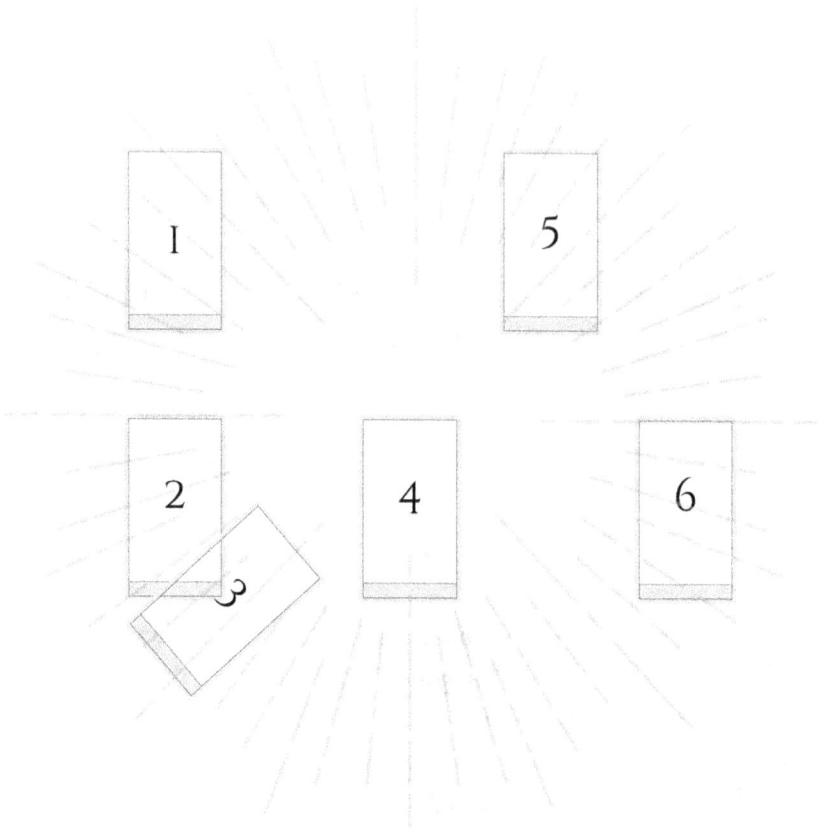

1. The vision for the project.
2. Its current state.
3. Something you're failing to recognize about the project.
4. Something you need to learn to move forward.
5. Your wider emotional life.
6. The next right thing.

AM I IN BURNOUT?

Burnout can be one of those things that sneaks up on an overwhelmed author. Because of this sneaky nature, it's easy to be too busy and preoccupied to notice it's actually happening until it gets out of control.

If you suspect you're heading for or maybe in burnout, draw this spread and get in touch with your energy levels and mental state.

1. Current energy status.
2. Current emotional state.
3. Fears.
4. What's driving you onward?
5. What's stopping you from resting?

OVERCOMING IMPOSTER SYNDROME

Imposter Syndrome looms large in just about every profession, but possibly more so in the creative fields.

Imposter Syndrome is that inner voice telling you that you're not worthy, that you're not qualified, that you don't belong. It's that voice in our heads that scoffs and questions, "who do you think you are, calling yourself a writer?"

Fortunately, Imposter Syndrome is a thought pattern that can be quietened and ignored. This spread asks you to think about the fears that fuel that negative voice and prompts you to look at your positive qualities that prove the inner critic is wrong.

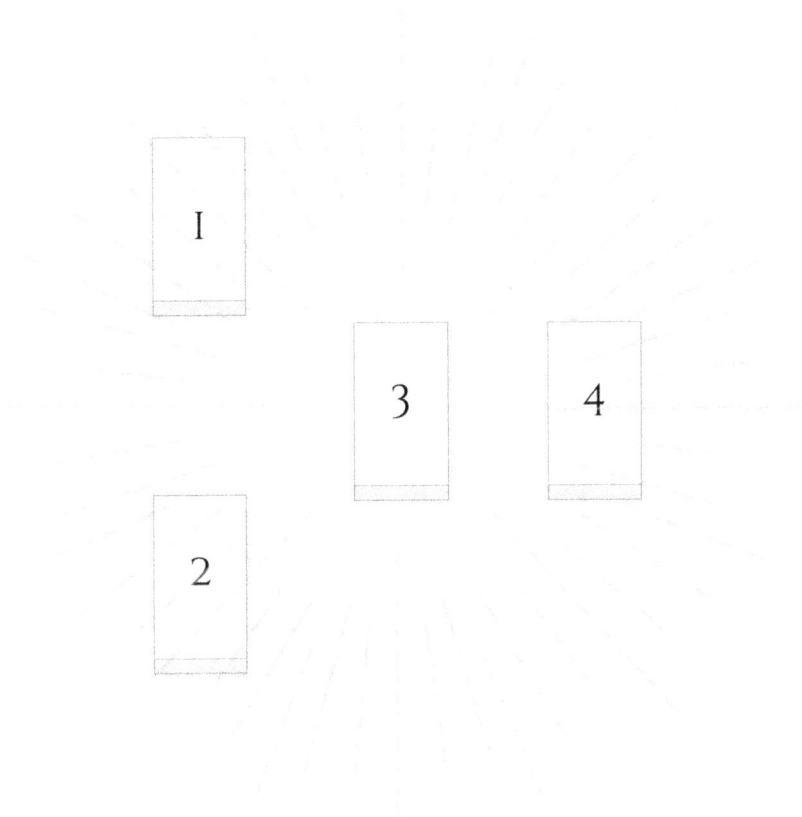

1. Your present state significator.
2. The root of the fear that makes you feel like an imposter.
3. The qualities that prove you're not an imposter.
4. Message toward self-acceptance.

BURNOUT RECOVERY

The demands of life are relentless. It's always been that way, but in our hyperactive world, that relentlessness has gone into overdrive. The result for many of us authors who are trying to keep up with the market, the industry, or even just our own ambitions is often burnout.

If you've identified you're in burnout, or have recently been burnt out, draw this spread to think about how to best recover.

1. Current energy.
2. Current emotional state.
3. Intuitive message from yourself.
4. The type of rest and replenishment you need.
5. What to do next.

AUTHOR CAREER OVERVIEW

An author career can come in as many forms as there are authors. There's no single way to define an author career, and even one author might go through many definitions of what a successful career means at different times.

If you're feeling adrift in your author life, unsure if you're on the right path, and wondering about your influences, or your motivations, this highly detailed spread can help unravel some thinking.

| 1 | 2 | 3 | | 4 | 5 | 6 |

9		10	11	12
8				
7		13	14	15

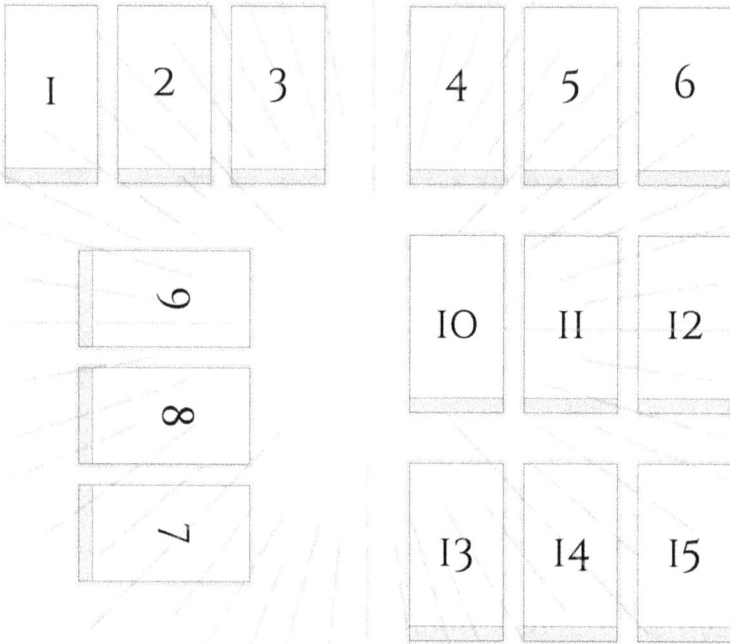

Present Factors

1. Significator.
2. Your current body of work.
3. Your overall vision of being an author.

Current Trajectory

4. Your daily work habits.
5. Your current work in progress.
6. Your current goals.

Alternative Path

7. A hidden desire.

8. An option you've previously dismissed.

9. An aspiration that seems out of reach.

Internal Influences

10. Fears.

11. A factor you're currently pleased with.

12. Intuitive advice.

External Influences

13. The publishing industry or market influences.

14. Your finances.

15. Your daily life.

CREATIVE MARKETING

Many authors run and hide at the prospect of marketing their work. But marketing doesn't need to be so scary!

Author marketing can be as much as a creative process as writing your book. This spread helps you look for ways to bring a creative sparkle to the marketing process by prompting you to think outside the usual patterns and examine your aspirations for your book.

1. How would you like to release this project into the world?
2. What marketing activities draw you and your current interests and skills?
3. What do you fear about marketing?
4. A marketing strategy or tactic you're not seeing.
5. Thing to do next.

INTUITIVE AUTHOR LIFE READING

Draw any number of cards while considering your author life in general. Let the cards speak to you freely. Don't consult any external guides.

What do the cards suggest?

SPREADS FOR
WRITING FICTION

SPREADS FOR CHARACTER DEVELOPMENT

DREAM SCENES

I love dream sequences in stories. Sure, they can be tricky to write well (which is why a lot of authors advise not to use them), but when executed with care, they can provide a fascinating glimpse into a character's subconscious. Dreams can define characters, and in certain stories, even direct an entire plot.

With its subconscious and metaphysical links, tarot is especially suited to inspiring dream sequences. Depending on which tarot deck you're using, the card's artistic symbology might directly transfer into your character's dreams.

1. Subconscious message.
2. Obvious conscious awareness.
3. Practical application of both messages.

WRITE TIP

Write a dream sequence however you choose, but be careful. A good practice is to always reveal to the reader when something is a dream. Be wary of starting a scene in a dream. If you do, make it short. Avoid the "it was all a dream" final ending. More often than not, these endings infuriate readers.

INSPIRING DIALOGUE

Dialogue does a lot of heavy lifting in a story. It is not only what the characters are saying, but it's also a tool of characterization and exposition. When characters are talking, there can be so much more happening than the information on the page. We also notice what the characters *aren't* saying.

This spread looks at the reasons for including a particular sequence of dialogue in the context of the wider scene, or even the entire story. It also examines the unspoken subtext of the conversation.

Add significator and relevance cards as appropriate for how many characters are in the scene.

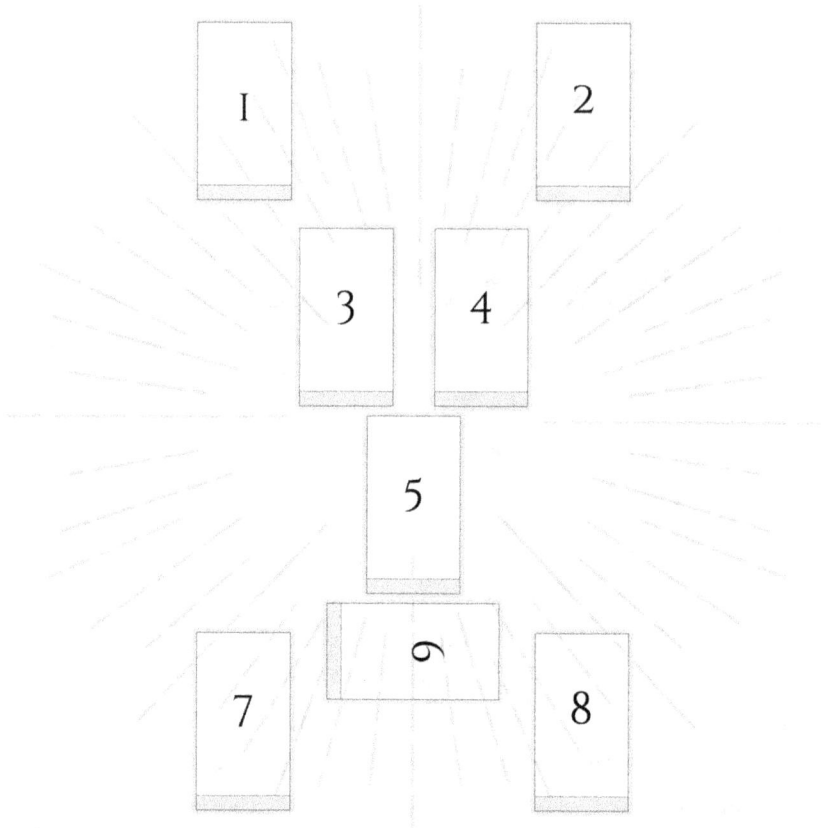

1. Significator for Character 1.
2. Significator for Character 2.
3. Goal of the conversation.
4. Goal of the scene.
5. What they are actually saying.
6. The unspoken subtext.
7. Relevance to overall character arc for character 1.
8. Relevance to overall character arc for character 2.

WRITE TIP

Dialogue should convey information to the reader, but beware info dumping through dialogue. Don't use dialogue to relay information to the reader that the characters themselves would obviously already know.

BASIC CHARACTER ARC

This spread examines the primary beats of a typical character arc. You can use it when developing characters or apply it retroactively to a character you've already written to help strengthen their arc in editing.

Add more helper character cards as your cast requires.

1. Starting significator.
2. Past.
3. Aspirations.
4. Blocks, obstacles, threats.
5. Fears.
6. Realization of past wounds.
7. The catalyst for them turning from reactive to active.
8. Helper character.
9. Character at the end.

CONFLICT RESOLUTION

While there are literary traditions that intentionally develop plots without conflict (see The Kishōtenketsu Spread), conflict is the lifeblood for most stories.

Conflict can manifest in different ways, but this spread focuses on interpersonal conflict between characters.

If you are working with more than two characters, add a card for each character's needs.

1. The needs of character one.
2. The needs of character two.
3. The middle ground compromise.
4. The outcome of accepting the middle ground compromise.
5. The outcome of refusing the middle ground compromise.

WRITE TIP /

Whichever outcome you follow, think about how that will cause further conflict, even if the conflict in this scene is resolved with a compromise.

CHARACTER GENDER EXPLORATION

Whether you're writing a gender binary or nonbinary character, considering how a gender spectrum manifests in any character is a way to add depth and nuance to your characterization.

Tarot is a useful tool in this thinking as many of the traditional cards depict gendered characters, e.g. The Emperor, The High Priestess, Queens, and Kings. These cards need not represent a specifically gendered person. Instead, they symbolize energies of archetypal male, female, or a harmony of the multiple.

1. Character significator.
2. Masculine.
3. Feminine.
4. Nonbinary.
5. Character by the end of the story.

WOUNDS AND GHOSTS

Much of what makes a character interesting, and a story worth reading, is centered around troubling things that have happened to them before the story started.

These past wounds, also called ghosts, are what our characters need to heal from. They provide the driving motivation for a lot of what our characters do and the decisions they make.

Use this spread to think about your character's previous hardships, and why they are relevant to what's happening within the plot.

1. Past event.
2. Person (besides the focus character) at the core of this past event.
3. Something the character doesn't see.
4. How this event manifests as the story starts.
5. Results from confronting this wound.

THE PURSUIT OF GOALS

A character's pursuit of their goals and how they are changed because of that pursuit over the course of the story is what makes a plot.

What does your character want? What do they need? Are they the same thing? What do they want in relationships? What do they want in their career? Do they have any competing or contrasting wants, needs, or goals?

You can perform this spread for any character in your story at whatever point. You can even do it for yourself.

1. Past hurts.
2. What the character wants.
3. What the character needs.
4. Character's chief obstacles.
5. Person whose help they need the most.
6. Next steps for them to reach their goal.

WRITE TIP

You can perform this spread for different spheres of your character's life and analyze how their different wants or needs might conflict. For example, what does your character want from their family life? What do they want from their career? Are those goals at odds?

CHARACTER'S LIFE VALUES

This intricate spread provides an overview of what a character thinks of their own life, according to fourteen central themes.

When drawing your cards, one for each theme, consider how the character values each one, or if they value them at all.

This spread is best used at the start of your writing project to create a solid character foundation to build on as you write. If you ever get stuck, this spread can also provide a way out of a block, providing context to help you decide what a character might do next.

The Character's Life Values spread is inspired by the Astrological Spread by Anna-Marie Ferguson as published in *A Keeper of Words*.

	I	
2		3
4	5	6
7	8	9	IO
II	I2	I3	I4	I5

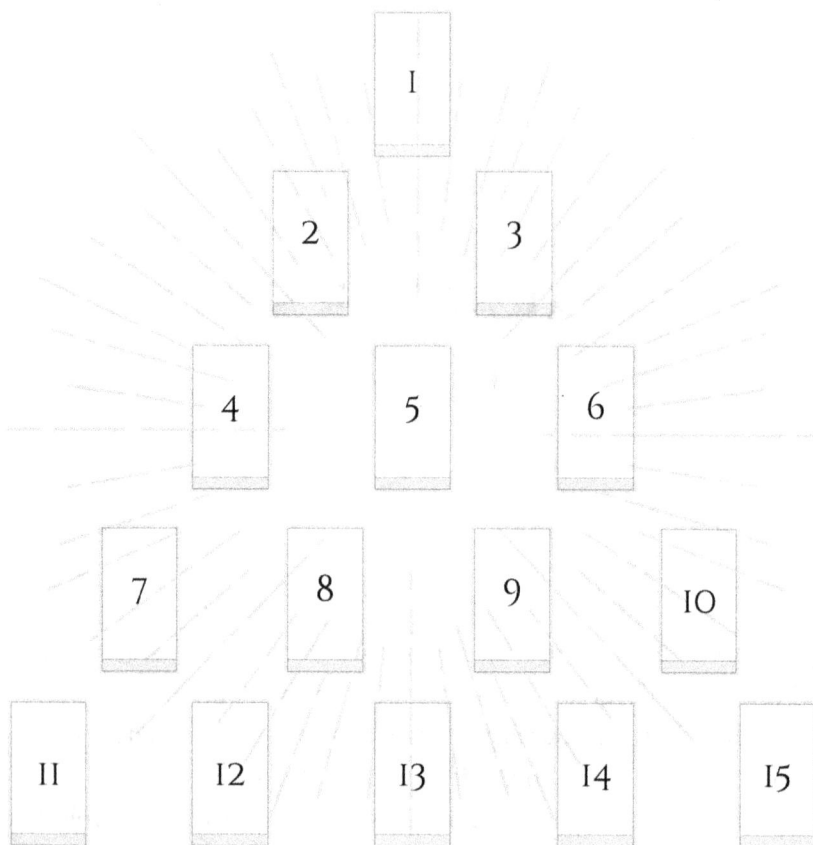

1. Personality, attitudes.
2. Finance and material matters.
3. Education.
4. Home, family, roots.
5. Creativity.
6. Leisure.
7. Work and career.
8. Health.
9. Romantic relationships.
10. Life cycles.
11. Religion.
12. Laws.

13. Ambitions, achievements, status.

14. Social life, friends and acquaintances.

15. Subconscious thinking, strengths, and weaknesses.

WRITE TIP

Not every detail you come up with here needs to go into the actual story. Sometimes these background particulars can serve the author in creating layered personalities without the reader needing to know the full history behind why a character is like they are in every regard. If you're creating a series, these extra details might reveal in later books and create deep continuity across your series.

EPIC INTUITIVE
CHARACTER OVERVIEW

This epic spread asks you to perform an intuitive reading for several significant life themes for your character. Put away your tarot guide books and anything else you might usually consult to discern a card's meaning, and trust your intuition to have a conversation with the card imagery.

This spread is similar to the Character Values spread. Where the former spread asked you to think about what the characters think, this time consider these themes of life from whatever angle the cards suggest. For example, the character's own values, the character's mother's opposing values, a societal value, etc.

Provide your own positions and labels for each thematic grouping of cards, or consider each theme as a whole. Read the cards as intuitively as possible.

How deep you go into this reading is up to you, but for central characters, you might want to spend some quality time with the ideas that arise.

This spread is such a useful exercise in considering an overview of life, you might even like to try it on your own life.

The Self

1.
2.
3.
4.

Home and Domestic Life

5.
6.
7.
8.

Work and Career

9.
10.
11.
12.

Relationships

13.
14.
15.
16.

The Future

17.
18.
19.
20.

WRITE TIP

Try free writing in your journal about what arises during this reading. You might even like to journal as if you are your character and perhaps even use these entries as character diaries in your story.

SOUL TRIPTYCHS

The soul triptych is a literary device that perceives a trio of characters as representing three facets of the soul: body, mind, and spirit. The three characters are individuals, but their contribution to a core group, the soul, is critical to the story as a whole.

Body - The body character is usually but not always physically strong, driven by passions and desires. The body is typically practical and concerned with the actual over the abstract.

Mind - The brain of the group. Often the one devising plans. Intellectual prowess. Strives for logic. Driven by clear rational thinking and sheer force of will.

Spirit - Driven by the heart when making decisions. The spirit is all about feeling.

A large cast might see several sets of characters all interacting as their own triptych sub-groups.

The following spreads prompt exploration of the soul triptych device in several ways.

Three Card Soul Triptych Spread

Draw one card for each, mind, heart, spirit.

Consider each card in relation to your associated characters. Alternatively, find inspiration for new characters in each card.

Triptychs Within Triptychs

Draw three cards for each element of the triptych. To add further depth to any character, you might like to consider how each character might embody different triptych elements along with their central role. For example, how might your heart character embody an element of spirit alongside their principal role?

Heart

Draw Three Cards

Body

Draw Three Cards

Soul

Draw Three Cards

WRITE TIP 🖋

Look around at other stories for the soul triptych character ensemble at work. Two popular examples are Harry Potter (Harry, Ron, Hermione - a basic trio with supporting characters), and Buffy the Vampire Slayer (Buffy, Willow, Xander - a core trio within an equally important ensemble cast including Giles, Angel, Spike, Dawn etc.).

PAST, FUTURE, PRESENT

I designed this life overview spread for characters in my novels, and yet have also found useful to apply my personal life. It looks at the ways we carry both the past and future with us in the present.

The position labels are deliberately ambiguous in order to inspire deeper intuitive interpretation and creative thinking.

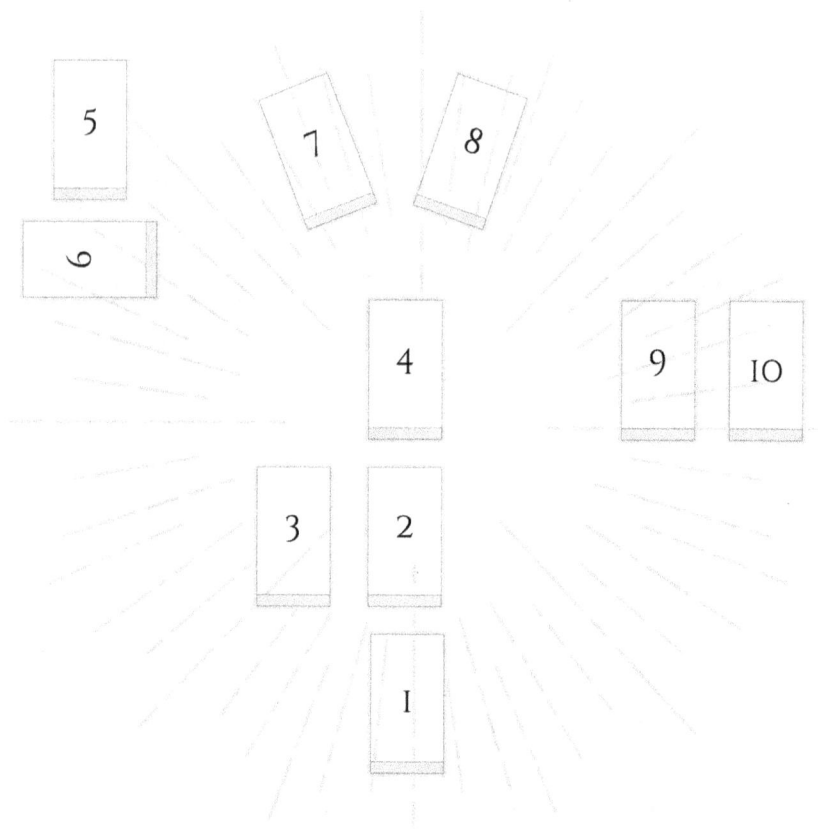

1. Questions that are hidden.
2. Root of desire.
3. Past paths.
4. Guiding ideals.
5. Current.
6. Past as present as future.
7. Impossible fantasies.
8. Realistic dreams.
9. Core intuitive theme.
10. Advice.

CHARACTER MIRROR

This quick spread considers how a character's internal world interacts with their external influences.

Use this in the outlining phase as you create your characters, or consult on the fly as you write and need to know what a character might do next.

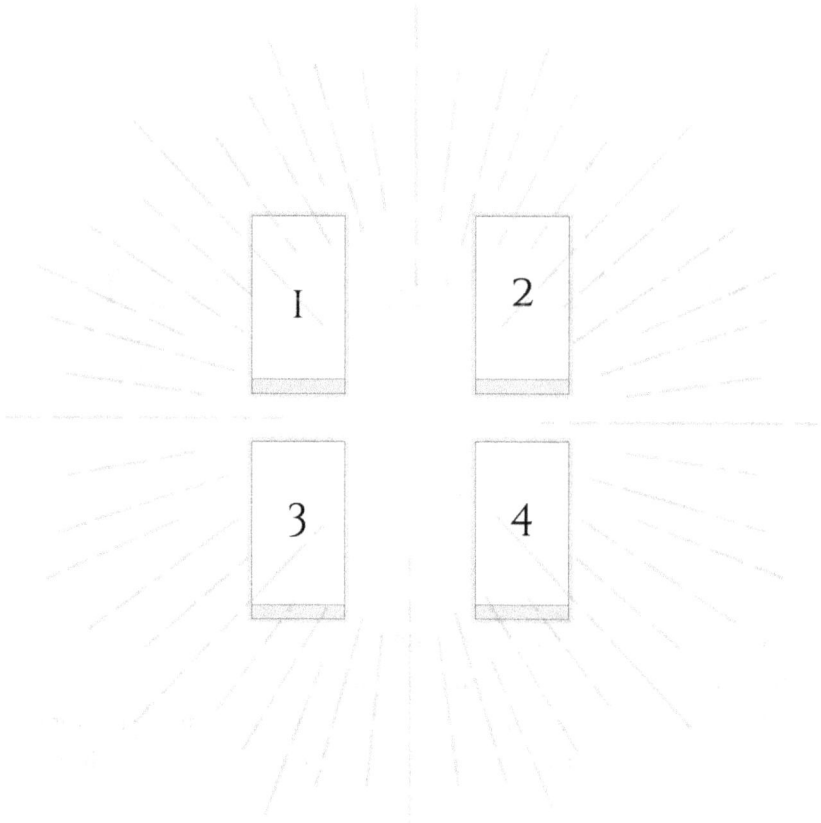

1. How the character perceives themselves.
2. How others perceive the character.
3. How the character perceives other's opinions of them.
4. A truth about themselves the character can't see.

WRITE TIP ✎

These perspectives can be useful for creating a general feel for how a character might act or react in a given circumstance, especially where other people are involved.

SIDE CHARACTERS

Sometimes a story requires a side character who is significant enough to necessitate some backstory and texture, but not so consequential that they need an in-depth character profile.

Use this spread to create a basic character overview for those supporting characters who don't warrant a whole life's worth of depth.

1. Past.
2. Present.
3. Future.
4. Significant life obstacle.
5. Significant life achievement.
6. Overall role in this story.

WRITE TIP

A side character is still a main character in their own life. Approach lesser characters with as much of a life as a main character, even though only a tiny slice of their experience will show up on the page. This is important if you're creating a series where these less prominent characters will recur.

GROUP DYNAMICS

In both fiction and real life, the way someone relates to others reveals their personality.

This can be in those highly charged dramatic moments we all love to read and write, be they negative or positive, or it can be in the simple ebbs and flow of daily life.

Use this spread to gather some insight about your characters and how they relate to others.

This spread is set up for an interaction between three characters. You can add or subtract characters as required for your work.

For a more detailed and complex spread, add three additional cards to the first 6 cards and read them intuitively.

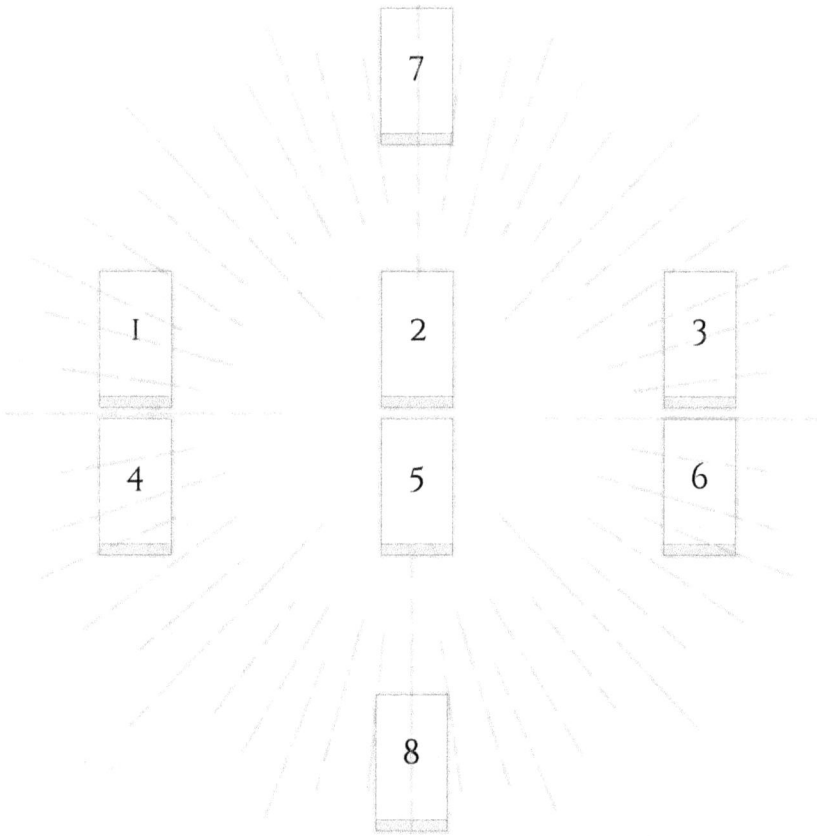

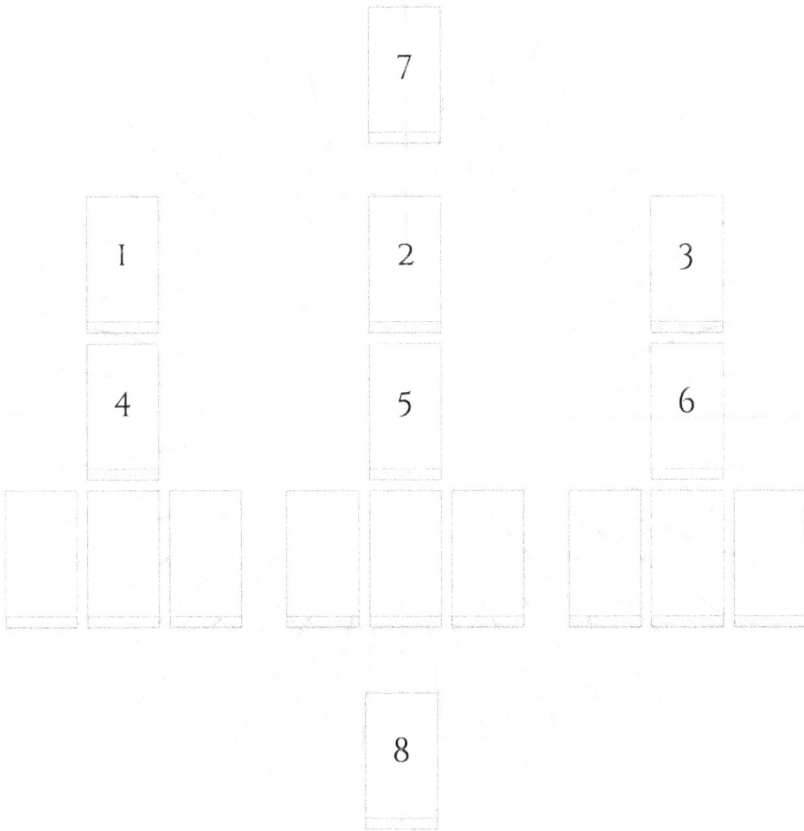

1. How Character A views the group (with optional +3 intuitive cards).
2. How Character B views the group (with optional +3 intuitive cards).
3. How Character C views the group (with optional +3 intuitive cards).
4. How Character A views themself (with optional +3 intuitive cards).
5. How Character B views themself (with optional +3 intuitive cards).
6. How Character C views themself (with optional +3 intuitive cards).

7. What is at stake in the interaction?
8. Hidden triggers within the interaction.

SETTING AS CHARACTER

A rich setting can function as a character in a story. Setting provides obstacles and solutions to your characters, and influences just about everything in the story.

Use this spread to explore your setting as a character, adding details and nuances you might never have otherwise considered.

1. Historical element about the place.
2. A secret about the place.
3. A commonly known aspect of the place.
4. How does this setting serve your character/s?
5. How does your character serve the setting?

WRITE TIP

To ensure your setting an integral part of your story, consider how your story could not have occurred in any other place.

CHARACTER FLAWS

Every character needs their shortcomings. This shouldn't be as superficial as "she was clumsy" or "he habitually overate." The character's flaw needs to be deep and harmful to themselves and or to others. Why? Because flaws create conflict and conflict creates story.

This spread follows a basic character sketch, looking at ways in which past events give rise to present negative traits. Cards should be interpreted in a negative context (it might be helpful to consider every card as a reversed meaning here).

1. Past events.
2. Current influences of past events.
3. Wound.
4. Manifestation of wound externally.
5. The wound as an obstacle.

FOUR SPREADS ABOUT ROMANCE AND RELATIONSHIPS

Whether you're writing a romance or weaving a romantic subplot into another genre, these spreads can help you explore your character's relationships, both as individuals and as a couple.

You can also apply these spreads to friendships, family connections, colleagues, and other platonic partnerships where the mutual interactions are critical to the plot.

INDIVIDUAL NEEDS

1. What the character perceives they want from the relationship.
2. What the character actually needs.
3. Past lessons from partnerships.
4. How ready are they to commit?
5. A significator card for their prospective partner who will provide the character what they need.

PARTNERSHIP BASICS

1. Character 1.
2. Character 2.
3. What brings them together.
4. What keeps them apart.

LESSONS TO LEARN

1. What partner 1 has to teach.
2. What partner 2 has to teach.
3. What partner 1 needs to learn.
4. What partner 2 needs to learn.
5. Outcome.

OVERCOMING DIFFERENCES

1. Character 1.
2. Character 2.
3. Commonalities.
4. Shared vision of the relationship.
5. Central theme of their conflict.
6. Compromise.
7. Moving forward together.

INTUITIVE CHARACTER READING

Draw any number of cards while considering your created characters in general. Let the cards speak to you freely. Don't consult any external guides.

What do the cards suggest?

SPREADS FOR PLOT DEVELOPMENT

CLASSIC FOUR ACT STRUCTURE - SIMPLE

The classic four act structure follows the pattern of a traditional three act structure, except we ensure that a defining midpoint shift occurs in the middle of the second act.

As such, you can see it as Act 1, Act 2a, Act 2b, Act 3.

This spread draws a card to encapsulate the central premise of each of the four acts.

1. Beginning.
2. Middle to the shift.
3. Turning point.
4. Resolution.

CLASSIC FOUR ACT STRUCTURE - ADVANCED

This complex spread follows the basic outline of the classic midpoint shift structure, but adds more opportunity to explore the nuances of the different acts.

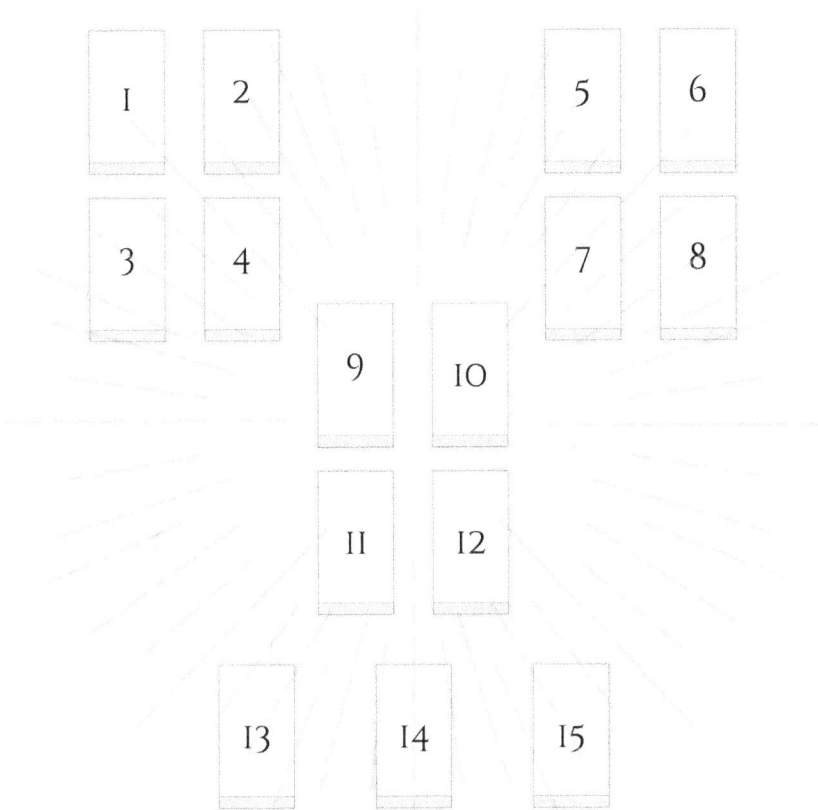

Beginning

1. Starting point.
2. Character's past.
3. Inciting incident.
4. A change the character sees they need to make.

Middle To The Shift

5. Character goes after something they want.
6. Obstacle.
7. Outcome after confrontation.

8. Fears.

Turning Point

9. A lesson.
10. Character's new position.
11. Obstacle.
12. What the character needs (not wants).

Resolution

13. Final Victory/Defeat.
14. Major lesson learned.
15. Conclusion.

KISHŌTENKETSU

Kishōtenketsu is a four act narrative structure developed within Korean, Chinese and Japanese traditions, originating in Chinese poetry.

Unlike most stories in the modern Western literary tradition, Kishōtenketsu is not based on cycles of conflict and resolution.

Each card in this spread represents one of the four acts of the Kishōtenketsu narrative structure. You can add more cards to each section to explore nuances in a more advanced reading if you wish.

1. Ki – Introduction
The character, setting, situation and other basic elements are established.

2. Shō – Development
An expansion of the first act introduction. No significant changes occur.

3. Ten – Twist
The story takes a turn into a contrasting, seemingly separate situation.

4. Ketsu – Conclusion

The story resolves, connecting all acts.

TAKE OFF YOUR PANTS

This spread is based on the story beats in Libbie Hawker's book, *Take Off Your Pants*.

The title refers to the popular naming of discovery writers as "pantsers" as they write by the figurative seat of their pants, to contrast with "plotters", those writers who outline.

Hawker's narrative structure is based on The Hero's Journey.

Draw one card for every story beat. You can also add clarifier cards for each position to prompt further details.

1. Opening scene.
2. Inciting event.
3. Character realizes external goal.
4. Display of flaw.
5. Drive for goal.
6. Antagonist revealed.
7. Thwart #1.
8. Revisiting flaw.
9. New drive for goal.
10. Antagonist attacks.

11. Thwart #2.
12. Changed goal.
13. Ally attacks.
14. Girding the loins (getting ready to launch the final attack).
15. Battle.
16. Death.
17. Outcome.

THE 3CS OF SCENE BUILDING

The 3Cs of scene building is a concept devised by author J. Thorn. It's based on the Five Commandments of Storytelling from Shawn Coyne's *The Story Grid*.

The 3Cs is a simple breakdown of a scene's structure as:

Conflict—something happens to move a character into action.

Choice—the character must choose to act one way or another (or not act at all).

Consequence—the results of the character's action.

Draw a card for each C of the scene.

1. Conflict.
2. Choice.
3. Consequence.

To advance the spread, draw additional clarifying cards for each C.

WRITE TIP

To create a cliffhanger scene, break the chapter or book before you reveal the consequence in the following chapter or book.

TURN THE SCENE

One method for constructing dynamic and compelling plots is to "turn the scene" from beginning to end.

This means to start a scene in one vibe and turn it to the opposite, or at least a competing situation, by the end of the scene. Examples are: character starts out hopeless and ends hopeful (or vice versa); a scene focuses on birth and ends in death (literal or figurative); starts in peace and ends in disharmony.

Consider a scene you're writing or editing and use this spread to think about ways it can be turned.

1. Scene start.
2. Significator for the most involved character.
3. Inciting incident to shift the scene.
4. Character's reaction as the catalyst of the scene shift.
5. Scene end, after the turn.

THEME BRAINSTORM

A story's theme can be a tricky thing to pin down, and often we can write entire novels without knowing what the theme is. However, knowing the theme before you set out, or developing it as you write your first draft, helps to create a more cohesive story with a succinct emotional impact.

Use this spread to think about different ways your theme might manifest in your story, both from your own intentions and from the journey your characters are going through.

1. Significator for the work.
2. Author's agenda.
3. Character's central challenge.
4. Character's overall outcome.
5. Lessons expressed in the work as a whole.
6. A general representation of the theme.

TINY MOMENTS ARC

Use this spread to inspire those small plot elements such as side threads or incidental scenes.

1. Beginning.
2. Middle.
3. End.
4. External element at the start of this arc.
5. External element at the conclusion of this arc.
6. Reason this small moment is important overall.

WRITE TIP

It can be quite satisfying for writer and reader to have a small scene or other seemingly insignificant moment end up influencing the entire story in some profound yet surprising way.

THE DARK NIGHT OF THE SOUL

In a traditional plot structure, a character typically goes through an "all is lost moment" just prior to the climax of the story. This is often called the Dark Night of The Soul.

At this stage, the character gives up in the face of seemingly insurmountable struggle.

How you interpret these cards will depend on where your story is heading. For example, a Happily Ever After romance novelist is going to read this spread differently to an Everything Is Doomed horror novelist.

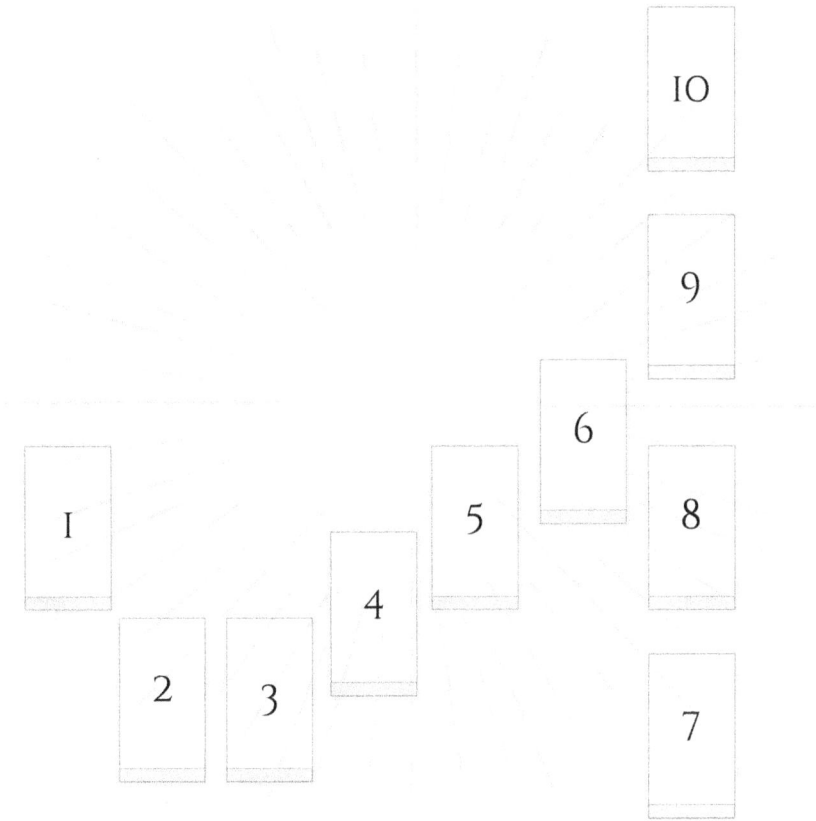

1. What leads to the dark?
2. The last obstacle that pushed the character to rock bottom.
3. What's really at stake?
4. A point of strength to cling to.
5. General emotional state that leads to this point.
6. A spark of wisdom from the character's intuition.
7. What's keeping the character in this dark state?
8. What do they have to accept to move forward?
9. The light at the end of the tunnel.
10. The way out.

WRITE TIP 🖋

If you're writing a positive and hopeful story, this Dark Moment can spark a revelatory moment for the character to shift them into a positive action.

If you're moving towards a more pessimistic ending, the Dark Moment is the beginning of the doomed end. This end may be more or less tragic than the all hope is lost dark moment.

WRITING OUT OF A CORNER

Sometimes the discovery writing process can lead to exciting and unexpected plot developments. Other times, it leads to frustrating dead ends.

If you've written yourself into a corner, try this spread to consider a variety of options on how to proceed. You can add further groupings of three cards to consider more than two paths if necessary.

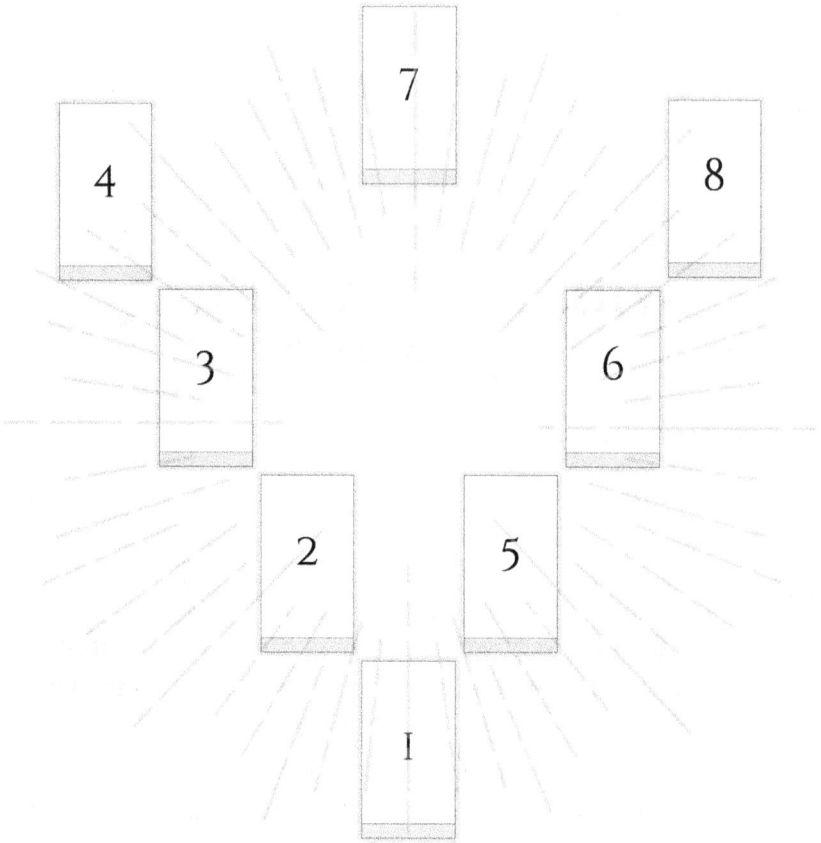

1. The truth behind the stuck situation.

Path 1

2. An opportunity.
3. A challenge.
4. The outcome.

Path 2

5. An opportunity.

6. A challenge.

7. The outcome.

8. The best way out.

CLASSIC ROMANCE BEATS

A typical romance novel follows a standard pattern of events that bring the couple together, force them apart, and bring them together again, and so on until their blissful union.

This spread is an overview of these basic romance story beats.

2	1		11	10
		12		
3				9
4				8
5			7	
		6		

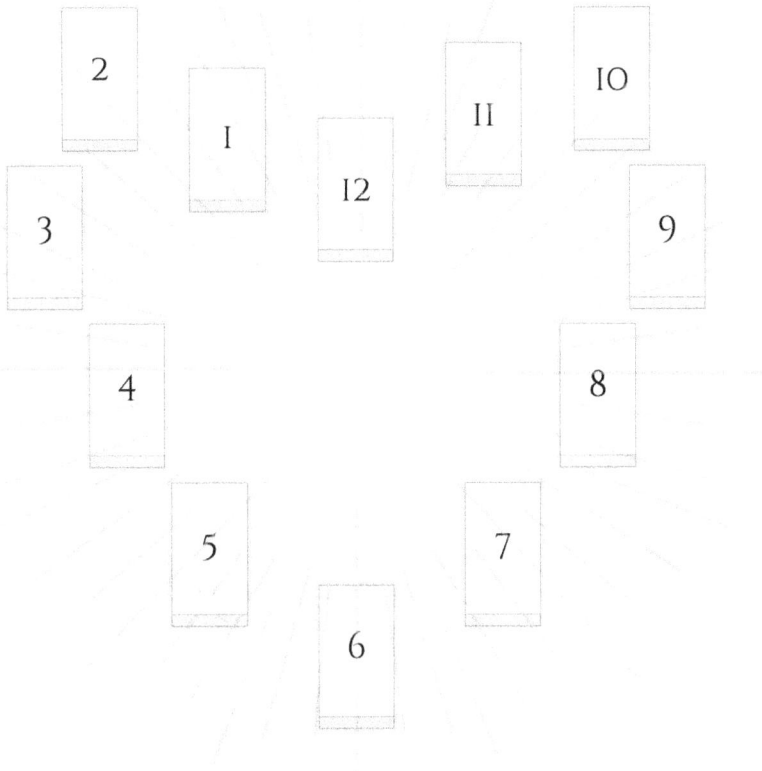

1. Character 1 starting significator.
2. Character 2 starting significator.
3. Meet cute.
4. Attraction.
5. Refusal of attraction.
6. Increased attraction.
7. Drawn together.
8. Commitment to union.
9. Questioning commitment.
10. Separation.
11. Grand gesture.
12. Happy ending.

CLASSIC HORROR BEATS

A horror story doesn't necessarily follow a series of genre defined beats like a romance novel does. There are, however, several defining structural characteristics of the genre.

This spread involves interpreting a card for each of these beats. Your interpretation will vary depending on what subgenre of horror you're working with. Some stories move toward hope, others to damnation. You can work through this spread with your pre-exiting subgenre in mind to guide your interpretation. Alternatively, you can use these choice moments as guides to what type of story to write and let the cards decide your subgenre.

1	
2	
3	
4	6
5	8 9
7	

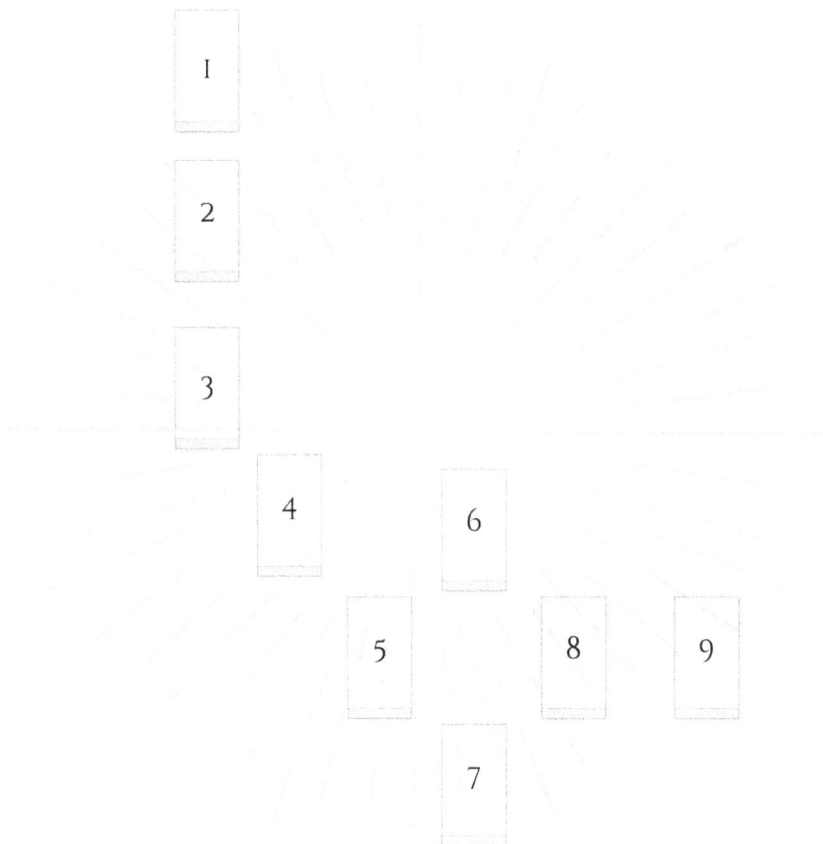

1. Normal world.
2. Inciting incident.
3. Problem intensifies.
4. Possible solution.
5. Peak terror.
6. Hope.
7. All is lost.
8. Hope restored (or all is doomed, depending on your subgenre).
9. The new normal.

Write Tip

The inciting incident can occur before the normal worlds is revealed and we learn what's at stake. This gives the opening normal world scenes an ominous overtone without the characters being aware anything is wrong.

CLASSIC MYSTERY BEATS

Mystery is another genre with a pre-established set of beats, but unlike some other clearly defined genres, mystery beats do not have to play out in a strict chronological order.

Use this spread to inspire the central beats of a mystery story. Add additional cards at position 7 for as many suspects as required.

```
        3   4
    2           5

  1                 6

                7
            8
        9

        10

        11


        12
```

1. Normal world.
2. Inciting incident.
3. Considering the mystery.
4. Launching the investigation.
5. Red herring.
6. Nature of clues.
7. Suspects.
8. All hope is lost.
9. The clinching clues.
10. Confrontation.
11. Revelation.
12. Return to the normal world.

YES, BUT; NO, AND

"Yes, But; No, And" is a way of thinking about progressive complications in a story as cycles of trying and failing. I borrow it from Mary Robinette Kowal and first heard her talk about it on the *Writing Excuses* podcast.

Here's how it works:

Your character is trying to achieve something.

YES, they achieve it...

BUT, something negative happens.

or

NO, they fail...

AND, something worse happens.

Structuring your action with "Yes, But; No, And" sequences provides compelling pacing, always moving the story forward.

When casting this spread, consider the scene you're trying to develop. Set the characters into their course of action. Do they succeed?

1. Yes.
2. No.

3. Which choice sequence is best for the story, Yes or No?
4. The resulting But.... or And... (Interpret depending on your choice from Card 3)

WRITE TIP

Combine sequences of "Yes, But" together with "No, And" to create an intriguing and compulsive read. Hold off revealing the resulting consequences (the Buts or Ands) until the following chapter or book to create cliffhanger scenes.

MAJOR EDIT CHECK IN

You've written a first draft and are now ready for your first major edit. Before you start, think about your first draft as a whole. You might like to read through it first before making any edits and then perform this spread to help guide your thinking.

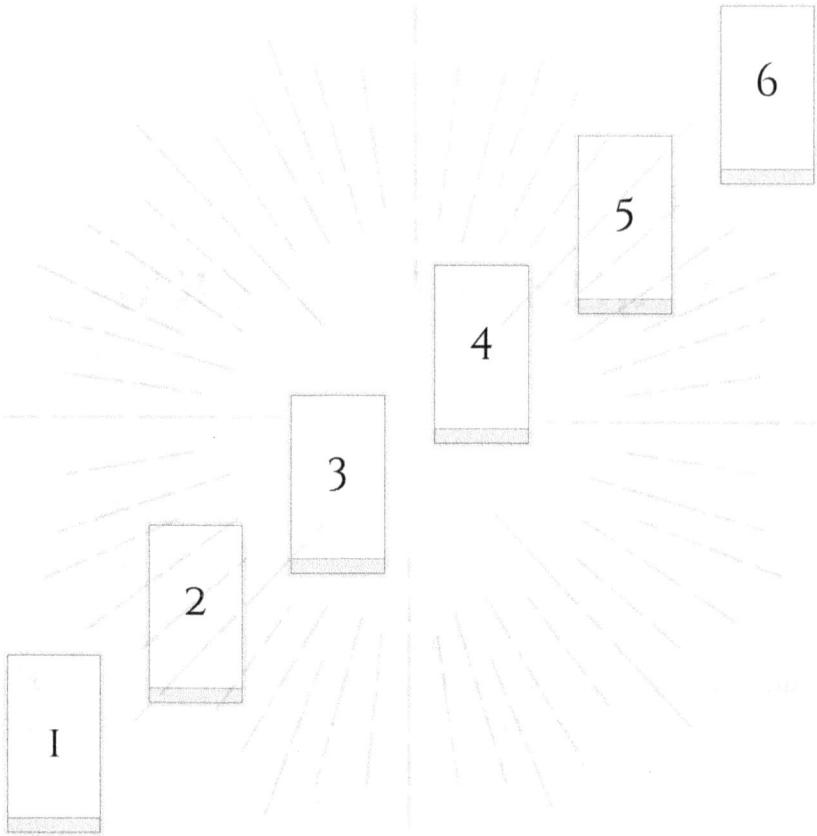

1. The current state of the first draft.
2. The work's key strengths.
3. Weaknesses.
4. Something that might need more time to think about.
5. Best direction from this point.
6. Overall goal or vision for the project.

INTUITIVE READING
FOR PLOTS

Draw any number of cards while considering your story plots in general. Let the cards speak to you freely. Don't consult any external guides.

What do the cards suggest?

SPREADS FOR NONFICTION

GATHERING IDEAS

Gathering ideas to brainstorm a nonfiction topic can be a similar process to that of writing fiction, however, typically nonfiction writing comes from a place of authority and sets out to solve a problem for the reader.

This spread focuses on these core features. It helps you discover your authority, or think deeper about what you already know. It then guides you to the most central problem that needs to be solved related to this topic. Read the third card position as intuitively as you can to explore how your authority connects to that problem.

1. Your current authority.
2. Core problem to be solved.
3. Your position in relation to the problem.

CREATING VALUE

Ideas for nonfiction are literarily everywhere. However, the most valuable ideas are those with a core meaning that inspire a change for the better, and have a wider world relevance.

This spread asks you to look beyond the basic idea gathering stage of brainstorming and prompts you to seek a central value for your work. What changes are you seeking to inspire in your reader? Why is this important to the wider world?

1. The core theme of your intended topic.
2. The change you're hoping to inspire in readers.
3. Why it's important?

AUTHOR INTENTION

Often a nonfiction author comes to their topic hoping to not only teach something to a reader, but to inspire learning and change in themselves.

This spread asks you to consider your motivation in writing your chosen topic. How do you hope to change the world? How to you hope to change yourself?

1. Why you want to write this piece.
2. Impact you hope to have on the world.
3. Lesson you hope to learn.

WRITE TIP

While nonfiction authors often write to teach themselves something, the reader is really only interested in how it all applies to them. Keep the reader and their problems in focus.

NONFICTION STORY STRUCTURE

Successful nonfiction writing tells a story as much as fiction does. We need to start from a position of lack, be presented with an idea that incites a desire to change. We need to know how to deal with prospective challenges, and what outcomes to expect.

This spread looks at the nonfiction narrative from beginning to end, covering problems to be solved and prospective solutions. The final card offers the reader a way forward as they finish reading and take your ideas off into their own lives.

1. Reader at the beginning.
2. Inciting change.
3. Challenges.
4. Turning points to aim for.
5. Resolutions.
6. The path forward.

FINDING A MEMOIR TOPIC

Memoir is an autobiographical account of an event that resulted in a profound change in your life. Like a fictional story, memoir structure echoes through the narrative of the Major Arcana. You start with the naivety of the Fool, progress through a series of challenge and enlightenments, to arrive to a knowing state.

This spread invites you to examine changes in your life, how you've grown by overcoming obstacles and learning lessons, and looks for themes that link these growth moments together.

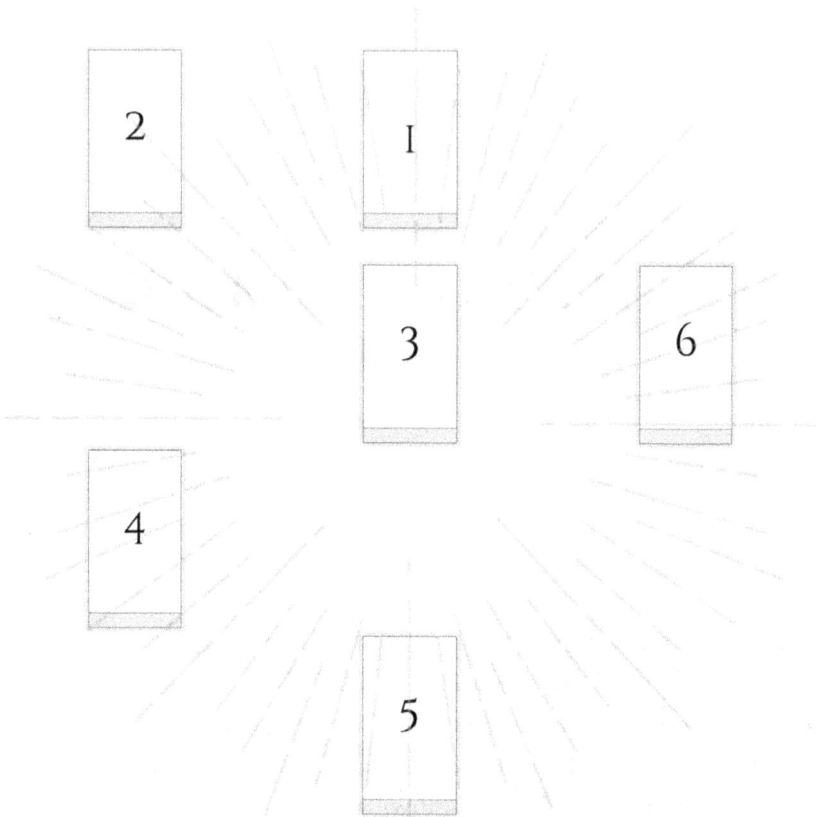

1. You now.
2. You past.
3. Something you know to be true in a profound sense.
4. A past event that shaped your knowing.
5. Something difficult.
6. A central theme drawing together positions 3, 4, 5.

NONFICTION WRITING PROMPTS

Use this simple spread as a writing prompt to brainstorm nonfiction topics. Look for inspiration not only in the meanings of the cards but also in the visual symbols used in the artwork.

1. A secret.
2. A profound lesson.
3. Your passion.

WRITE TIP ✒

This prompt sequence also works well for finding fiction ideas.

EXTERNAL IDEAS

This spread asks you to look outward for an idea. How does that external issue relate to you personally, and how might you help someone else who is connected to this same issue?

1. A current event in the world.
2. You in the present.
3. Something you know about position 1 that might help someone.
4. Angle for topic to draw 1, 2, 3 together.

SELF-KNOWLEDGE TO STRENGTHEN IDEAS

This spread asks you to consider core things about yourself you know to be true and how they improve ideas or arguments you are writing about. The card position labels have been made intentionally open to inspire creative interpretation and intuitive reading.

1. Confidence.
2. Adversity.
3. The path.
4. Balance.
5. Zeitgeist.
6. Reward.

INTUITIVE NONFICTION READING

Draw any number of cards while considering your created characters in general. Let the cards speak to you freely. Don't consult any external guides.

What do the cards suggest?

How to Develop Your Own Tarot Spreads for Writing

As you continue to inspire and explore your writing life with tarot, you might like to develop new spreads for your specific requirements.

Like all work we do with tarot, this is a process of what feels right to you in the moment.

Find some quiet, solitary time, and shuffle your deck while you consider the aspect of your writing life you want to explore.

What are the key components of this situation?

What are the fundamental questions you have?

Are you seeking an ultimate answer or just some musings to inspire you?

You can determine how many cards to draw before you start the spread, perhaps figuring them out first in your tarot journal. You might also lay the cards as it comes to you in the moment and see how it all feels.

Like some spreads in this book, your card arrangements can be symbolic. For example, cards looking to the future might be on the right (as we read progressively left to right in English). Or an overarching concern might sit at the top of a spread. Consider the ladder section of the traditional Celtic Cross spread that sees the final four cards read upward toward the outcome card as though you are climbing through the reading. Have fun and get creative with the arrangements of your cards.

You might like to return to your custom spreads again, so make sure you note down what each card position means.

Ultimately, the position of the cards does not really matter. It's just another layer of symbolism we can add to the tarot reading, another way to inspire a creative practice, and another aspect of tarot reading that is entirely up to you as to how and why you do it in a certain way. Trust yourself.

YOUR TAROT JOURNEY

Tarot is a lifelong exploration. There will never be an ultimate moment when you learn everything the cards can teach you. There will always be more meaning, more intuition colored by your ongoing experience, and more decks to explore. I believe this is why so many practitioners (myself included) end up owning so many decks.

A spread cast on one day may mean something totally different the next day, even if you read with the same cards.

As you continue your readings too, watch out for recurring cards. This happens to a lot of practitioners (myself included) where the same cards show up in different readings, even across different decks. It could be a coincidence, but it certainly feels like magic.

It's okay to believe this is something otherworldly speaking to you through the cards. It's okay to believe it's a total coincidence. It's okay to be a casual tarot user, dabbling with the cards whenever you feel like it. It's okay to become a completely absorbed tarot enthu-siast and let the cards permeate your life on every level. It's okay to never learn the traditional meanings of the cards, and it's okay to always consult the tarot guidebooks and never memorize meanings or read with your intuition.

Just as the writing world means something different to every writer, tarot is yours to use and play with as you need.

Enjoy your journey.

CONSULTED WRITING RESOURCES

These writing resources were consulted in the development of this book.

Coyne, Shawn. *The Story Grid: What Good Editors Know*. Black Irish Entertainment. 2015.

Cron, Lisa. *Story Genius: How To Use Brain Science To Go Beyond Outlining And Write A Riveting Novel*. Ten Speed Press. 2016.

Hawker, Libbie. *Take off Your Pants: Outline Your Books For Faster, Better Writing*. CreateSpace Independent Publishing. 2015.

McKee, Robert. *Story: Substance, Structure, Style and the Principles of Screenwriting*. Regan Books. 1997.

Thorn, J. *Three Story Method: Writing Scenes*. J Thorn. 2022.

Writing Excuses Podcast. www.writingexcuses.com

TAROT MEANINGS FOR WRITERS

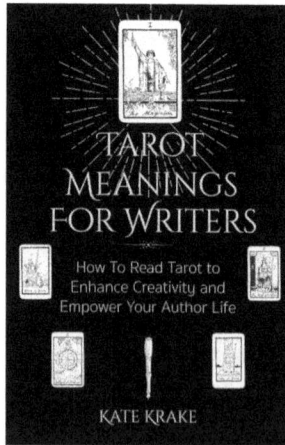

You don't need generic tarot interpretations.
You need meanings that speak directly to your writing life.

Tarot Meanings For Writers explores all seventy-eight cards through the lens of creativity, writer psychology, emotional blocks, breakthroughs, and artistic growth.

Every card is translated specifically for authors.

Use it to interpret your spreads.
Use it to understand your patterns.
Use it to deepen your symbolic thinking.

Get *Tarot Meanings For Writers* and step into a richer understanding of your creative patterns.

Available in ebook, print, and audiobook.

About the Author

Kate Krake writes magical and otherworldly fiction, as well as personal and creative development for writers.

She is passionate about folklore, art, pop culture, long distance walking, tarot, and curious trivia. She can usually be found with her nose in a book, her ears in a song, and her head in the clouds.

Kate has lived all over Australia and currently lives in Perth, Australia, with her family.

Connect

www.katekrake.com
kate@katekrake.com

BOOKS BY KATE KRAKE

FICTION

Night Shift At The Shadow Bay Hotel

THE WITCH AGAINST WICKED SERIES

A Maze of Murder

A Mask of Chaos

A Trial of Ghosts

A Wreath of Ruin

A Hex of Wolves

A Trick of Terror

A Coven of Demons

SHORT STORY COLLECTIONS

Creatures of The Liminal Wilds: Speculative Stories of Bewildering Beasts

Familiar Shadows of The Strange: Stories of Psychological Surrealism

NONFICTION

THE CREATIVE WRITING LIFE

A Writer's Creativity

A Writer's Practice

A Writer's Mindset

The Creative Rebellion

Journaling For Writers

How To Be A Better Writer

Write Your Novel In A Month

How To Write Your First Novel

Writing Beyond Fear

<u>The Writer's Book of Joy</u>

<u>The Writer's Book of Weird</u>

TAROT WRITERS

Tarot For Writers

Tarot Spreads For Writers

Tarot Meanings For Writers

Author Arcana: A Tarot Journal For Writers

Inkwell & Elm

Inkwell & Elm publishes premium resources to help writers and other creatives achieve success.

THE INKWELL & ELM GROUP

The Creative Writing Life

Tarot Writers

Writing Prompt World

www.ingramcontent.com/pod-product-compliance
Lightning Source LLC
Chambersburg PA
CBHW072245270326

41930CB00010B/2270